I0756244

FINISHING LINE PRESS
www.finishinglinepress.com

Paddling the Sweet Spot Between Life and Death

poems by

Laura E. Garrard

Finishing Line Press
Georgetown, Kentucky

Paddling the Sweet Spot Between Life and Death

for Mike, my family,
the prayer angels,
and people living/dying with cancer

ISBN 979-8-89990-381-6 First Edition

ACKNOWLEDGMENTS

I gratefully acknowledge the editors and publishers of the publications where these poems first appeared:

"Paddling the Sweet Spot," *Tidepools*
"My Body Speaks," "I Can't Go Back," "Does Grief Die?" "Stigmatized and Written Off," "The More Minutes I Find Prismatic, the Less Dark My Attic," *OncoLink.org*
"The Only Else There Is, The Breath," *PicturesOfPoets.org*
"Humbled," *The Paddock Review*
"The Walk," "Sailing in the Sunshine," *Potpourri: Poetry–Prose–Pictures*
"I'm Not the Heroine of Your Cancer Novel," *TulipTree Review: Wild Women*
"What Can I Say About Eating Raisins During the Storm?" "Elegy to a Cancer Altar," *Amethyst Review*
"Filled to the Brim," *Thin Places & Sacred Spaces*
"Homage to My Radiated Hip," Finalist, John & Eileen Allman Prize for Poetry, *Bellevue Literary Review*
"My Mother's Parents Free Ranged," *The Madrona Project: The Empty Bowl Cookbook*
"Salmon Parenting," Inspired by *Art: Olympic Peninsula Authors & Artists*
"Hugging Alder," Merit Prize Winner and Pushcart Prize nominee, *TulipTree Review: Stories That Need to be Told 2024*

Publisher: Leah Huete de Maines
Editor: Christen Kincaid
Cover Art: Laura E. Garrard
Author Photo: Amy Collett
Cover Design: Elizabeth Maines McCleavy

Order online: www.finishinglinepress.com
also available on amazon.com

Author inquiries and mail orders:
Finishing Line Press
PO Box 1626
Georgetown, Kentucky 40324
USA

Contents

Paddling the Sweet Spot

Starting with deep powerful strokes
Direct your paddleboard on a diagonal
In between the edges of waves,
The sweet spot not easy to maintain.

When you've found that rhythm
A meditative state claims you.
You glide faster with ease,
Meld into the narrow exception

Of movement against the current,
Making headway until you notice
You're in the sweet spot,
Veer slightly, then lose it.

My Body Speaks

I ask my body why it has a tumor—
Why not go to the source?
I listen, write in stream of consciousness.
She tells me I was under stress,
Gave away too much of myself in order
To receive love, honor, and respect.

I ask my body what she needs,
She says to get more rest and do less.
Now, this is difficult.
When I immerse, I want to excel—
Do more than my best,
To hell with rest.
Rest is dull,
Rest is dying.

My body says rest is recovery—
Recline until you feel satisfied
Like a big yawn after a nap,
There's nothing in that still moment
Besides recognizing yourself.

I ask my body what I am
Supposed to be in this life.
She says to be myself,
Create art from the place of rest
And it will be transformative.

The Only Else There Is, The Breath

1.
Crying   Oh God
You have to heal me.
On my shins again.
I seem to get better, but then
A test says otherwise.
I am lost in this world of tests
For which I cannot prepare.
I'm living a nightmare naked at my desk.
It's the way things are out of my hands
That make it unclear how to progress.

Would you have me shrink away to nothing?
A slow death toward eventual crown?
What is the honor in that?
What is a human without honor?
Don't you see me suffering?
How can you leave me to ask what's next
With health outside my grasp?

2.
My pleadings don't get me anywhere
But up again.
As I come off the cold brick,
Tears drying, sobs subsiding, I stand.
I move, let my body do what it still can
And feel blood return to my heartbreak,
Pump by pump, breath by breath.
In the midnight silence of no answers
I stop the questions and begin Qi Gong.

3.

The only else there is

To keep being human

Through moving   hope

To find the me

To whom I return

Again and again

After I give her up

I pick her back up

Cradle her lostness

In hands rising and falling

With the breath

I give her flow

To recollect

What it is like

To feel whole

Humbled

I am cleaved by lightning.
Bared of bark, my proud
Leaves, trimmed limbs.
Burned to minimal—
Survival instinct.

But my roots stick,
Sustain decisions,
Ground me to forces
Subterranean—
The cleansing undercurrent,
Joy.

The material and mundane
Fade to fall.
Dropped are prescribed priorities.
I bundle what
Humility has hewn,
Release into the Storm

Day by day, engage primary growth
That reflects necessary change
According to no plan,
A revival in present-minded
Shade.

The Walk

Tall striking beauty
Brandishing new
Pink ribbon sneakers
Countenance of a tree
She glances toward me
Then focuses directly

A breadth of exchange appears
In her bathed brown eyes
Recognize myself weeks ago
Scared   strong   in fear
Clear   near tears

The unknown has hit
The big leveler
Death inviter
Life challenger

Out of her experience
Out of her control
Swing set emotion
Up to down to up
Turning up the compost
Bringing up the rot
Mixing rich earth
With decomposing parts

Powerful long treads
Torso and head
Leaning their best
To stay in stride
With feet and legs

She walks with dignity
Desperation
Because she knows
That her present and future
Are in constant question

And she's trying to flow
In the healing experience
Be brave
Not relinquish
Living is precious
The trick is
Not wanting it too much
Not calling death closer

There's the rotting rub
How to survive
Remain oneself
Be the gracious woman
You've learned to be
Without handing your life
Body and self-sufficiency
Over to those who
Have no idea who you are
Or what you contribute
To your world

Most patients discover
There is no advocate
But the woman
In the mirror

The life preserving
And altering decisions
Are hers to endure

I smile at her
With transparency
Knowing encouragement

For I'm in it too
Just a different side of the path
Recognition shines in her eyes
She knows my plight is hers
She's not alone on this walk

Stigmatized and Written Off

Three close friends of mine opt out.
The last thing said, It's treatable right?
Yesterday I read an athlete obit,
Younger man dies in a kayak accident.
So alive was he, everyone in shock,
His abrupt memorial packed no doubt.
But what of those who linger on?

Letting go is a large lesson
In life and death facing.
There's almost an inward scoff,
No more energy for outward response
To those unconsciously saying,
Sorry that you've got cancer cells
Running all over your body,
Or, So, you're going to do the
Killing yourself thing to live.
Yes, these things are said.
Surprised? By ignorance,
False confidence, in a culture
That worships youth and wealth?
Well, I don't plan to die just yet—
Is that okay with you?
And not every subsequent health issue
Is another cancer—Sorry,
Does this disappoint your need
To assume that for me it's all over?

I'm folding myself into poetry batter,
Yes, writing myself in
For whatever time I have to spend,
And with those friends who
Will have me outlive them.
Dumped due to an impending death—
You're damn right I care about that.
Aren't we all headed that way?
Most don't deny and set me aside.
I thank God for this every day.

Some Days, I Grieve Your Grief

I do not believe I will die soon.
Yet I grieve that you may lose sleep,
Gulp when my absence
Guts you in public,
Or sink into your heart pit when
You hear our song.

I'm a sap, empathy overachiever,
Still this final thought for you—
Don't spend precious time thinking
I should have lived longer, done this or that.
When you retrieve me, know I'm still here,
Not a ghost but a favorite color
Woven into your wool sweater.

Remember when our border collie
Would not let me grieve him?
When wanting him welled my throat
I heard a whisper,
I'm heeling beside you.
His shadow warmed my leg,
A shrug grew in sadness' stead,
I petted his eidolon head.

Let my sentience stay for you
And not interfere with your future.
When that unfathomable tear
Threatens to unravel the thread,
Breathe into your chest,
Smile if you can.
Pat your shoulder as my hand.
I am here now
And will be then.

I'm Not the Heroine of Your Cancer Novel

I won't star in your after-school special,
You expect me to fill your courage bill,
Want the gory chemo details,
The rancid toilet, the clichés?
Not every patient pukes after treatment
Nor loses their hair, and one who has, says to me
Thank God, you don't need to share such stories,
If you did, I would puke again from the mere mention.
He doesn't wear these passage rites as banners.

You trigger my trauma,
Mind and body flooded so
I can't talk, only tremble,
Can't think clearly for hours
After you challenge me in class,
Write this poem as if speaking to Cancer.
You don't hold the right to decide
Where and when I should overcome
Because you think me strong.
I need strength to soothe more important shocks.
Though how can you know this is wrong,
Our culture wants cancer heroes, survivors
Of these diseases beyond our control.
I don't take it personally, really, but my body does.

Cancer realities are not dramas
To raise up as martyrs.
These words are not meant to inspire leaders,
They seek to resonate, embalm little wisdoms
That seep from beyond the grave,
Share hard-earned humility and advocacy,
Admit honest low moments, proffer hope.
Many patients and docs will tell you
Cancer paths walk largely in the head and heart—
Stress over diagnoses, and yes treatments,
Fear about death.

If you want more bile in your book,
Volunteer on an infusion wing of
Traditional hard-hitting chemotherapy.
Thankfully, I've not piped it into

My petite, hard-to-poke veins
Because I know this body won't take it.
I stop immunotherapy infusions as soon as
Veins object by turning red afterward,
And I show a safe level of improvement.
Complete remission isn't always achieved,
Instead I follow this body's needs and signals
As gently as able, live faithful to instinct,
Support my most successful survival,
Keep what's working of my own immune system
As long as possible.

One doctor says he cures myeloma, (a 30-40% chance of)
Suggests I start with traditional chemo—
The possible effects, including death,
Blur my vision just reading about them—
Then three rounds of four drugs, a double,
Meaning dying twice, bone marrow transplant
That first kills your entire blood system,
Replaced by stem cell reintroduction
While at risk of fatal infection,
Followed by three years of the initial four drugs.
He says, You're young, you'll do well—No, I just can't do it,
Know I'll die from these treatments.
Decide to rely on scientific research,
Control disease by least intervention
Needed to sustain quality-lived life.
New drugs are on the rise.

I'm not in a battle with cancer,
I'm enduring to heal my mind-body,
So don't misappropriate my story,
If it's macabre and victory you want,
Read a war novel.
I may never win your cancer-free ribbon,
Yet my pages still turn.

I Will Welcome That Type of Trouble

1.
At the brink of complete frustration, I yell
Because there's no one to hear.
I mean, full on, scraping the fear
From every cell kind of yelling.
I'm so sick and, yes, tired of this—
I feel alone in this.
I'm not, it's just I'm the one
Who must really deal with it—
The endless blood draws, side effects.
Sometimes there are none
But then here it comes,
The reality of low immunity
And the lack of certainty.

May I have normal troubles?
Of course, the normal may no longer trouble.
This morning I feel old hurt remnants
Vacate my entrails due to the yell decibel.
I get the feeling there's no going back,
This path is one that changes everything,
All perceptions about living
Because my horizon could black hole me
Like a mailed Flat Stanley.
I must plump my life
With red rich experiences,
I refuse to settle for sickness.

2.
Tired of lab vampires, bless them.
I have a friend who cannot stand needles,
Cannot imagine what this would be like for her.
I no longer ask Why Me, believe most
Will not escape this plague called cancer.
It's Earth's calling card to our selfishness,
To the beings out of balance.
Disease has a way of cleaning up trouble.
I'm just one of the many,
Yet I'm someone's loved one,
Also a patient to a hematologist—

He has a name and so do I.
He writes me back in my portal (Oh God).
I cannot imagine what it's like to be him,
Working with those who may or may not survive.

3.
What are my troubles to this world?
They matter only to those who love me.
Why will I survive but to be with them?
In the end what's more important than
Friends who celebrate me living?

I have no children for whom I'm responsible,
Lucky me. I have a husband, family,
But they take care of themselves—
This takes a little off the edge of death, I perceive.
My incentive is to see what happens next,
To see where God leads me.
After I become stronger
Life could continue in a way
Very unexpected. Life after cancer—
Now that's an adventure worth it.

I've already dealt with the worst,
Shock, grief, death of profession,
Loss of physical health, friends & freedom.
Will unsubstantial worries worm into
A more mundane every day?
Ha, yeah, one can hope. My apple
Will welcome that type of trouble—
I dare the petty to penetrate.
However I've discovered
Nothing about living is petty.

I Surrender All

Just off the path,
I notice a caterpillar
Affixed to the axis of a fern frond.
It seems to have died while eating,
Gorged in bountiful summer green.
Toward end, did it miss losing time
To grow powerful wings?
Is it too late to soar, have I
Done all I will do, become?

Peace flies into regret
When I finally accept
The finality of death.
Not that I don't believe
In continuance.
It's just that this physical
Sheath and its incompletion
Will loosen me one day.
When that happens,
I won't grasp what is unfinished.
Therefore, why fight against
Death as if it were a foe?

Return to the table of body and blood.
Remember that He lives in me—no matter how long.
Breathe deeply and sacrifice
The fight, the flight, into absolution.

The human spirit struggles
With letting go into the larger.
We strive for individual meaning
When in the end, we dissolve into
What we cannot yet fathom.
There, we won't care about this cocoon
Existence, youthful wishes.
We are the dream,
It doesn't spin us.

What Can I Say About Eating Raisins During the Storm?

I'm not confident
    the storm's end has come.
It hasn't flattened my home
    nor tattered my hope.
All will ride the rainbow
   to the other side,
We don't know when.
The present wind,
    no matter
    direction
    is now my friend.
None of us controls weather
    and fear is a lying dictator.
Let my master be the one
    who's always been there with me
    even in the dismantling.
Living on the edge, I look directly into the sun.

The More Minutes I Find Prismatic, the Less Dark My Attic

When I turned thirty, I lamented to an older friend that I had not yet married or started a family. I whined, I am ready for my life to begin. He asked me something I've not forgotten, 'Have you considered that this *is* your life?' Always goaling forward, I did not adopt this viewpoint. I was the ultimate checklist crosser off-er, the what's-next discontented.

It took a cancer crisis to develop internal infrared vision and see life in the dark. Life doesn't begin after certain things happen. Life won't start again when I'm well. It's happening right now no matter my waiting for an 'all clear' or a death knell.

I would be wise to notice the brilliance in motion: an ekphrastic rainbow framing the mountain-bordered lake, a wisp of blond hair falling onto my husband's face, a pair of bald eagles circling thermals above my head, and sunshine illuminating the black pearls in my chest.

I don't know what the box of survival chance holds. Future focus deprives me of this moment. Should my life be shortened, I don't want to miss my everyday birth presents. I want to live the happiest I can *now* even when not knowing that everything is going to be okay. And I need only laugh deeply to define what's essential—spontaneous eruptive joys that rinse my mind of uncertainty and radiate worry within me.

Elegy to a Cancer Altar

After my diagnosis we moved West.
I set an altar in our living room
overlooking Lake Crescent.
For over two years I knelt here
staring at an apex of Creation.
Outside waves chewed my pain.
I longed for deep breaths, release of
resistance: pushed aside tears, the buried.

On the pine table I placed
dried sage in an abalone shell,
rattles, a drum, pipe tobacco.
Tools to petition, focus thought
toward Spirit, Inner Self.
Also, gifts of encouragement
in stones, charms, totems.

A leather medicine sac
held a miracle ice-blue crystal
once curbing the backache
of my friend Ray,
offered to my palms in ceremony
before my bone marrow biopsy.

Another pouch, yarn woven,
contained consecrated eagle ash
bestowed by a half-Cheyenne sister.
I carried this to the Clinic in Rochester
& rubbed animal powder
on the hip that housed a tumor.

Plus, grandmother's wooden round
case shrouding a silver cross,
a heart-shaped rattle from my doctor,
quartz elephant from a healed client,
prayer beads from my mother.

These symbols of care
formed a semicircle
atop a handsewn table runner

of eight colors, a chakra
rainbow undertow.

Often I touched the tokens
in relieving lamentation,
to sense family and friends,
support constant & surrounding.

And prayed by opening
the Four Directions,
lit bundled sage to smudge
the ions around my feet,
legs & hips,
torso, arms, head.
My energy extended.

I connected to Grandfather above,
Son & Mother, Mary Magdalene,
spiritual helpers. Earth's wisdom,
elements & nourishment.
And All Relations who fly, crawl,
swim, stand & walk.
My light swelled in company.

I pinched sweet smelling tobacco
between index and thumb,
pierced it with tribute,
appeals for healing,
entreaties for kin,
our floundering civilization.
Then burned all on the shell,
smoke litany to Sky.

These pleas moved within me,
strengthened & blessed
my body, cleansed fear
& internal yelling.

One day, I examined the altar
& knew it was time to dismantle.
Tenderly tucked the keepsakes

into boxes, washed the ash
from the technicolor dream cloth,
folded & laid it in cedar.

Despair has departed these mementoes,
their purport stowed alongside hope,
the emotion now invoked when
I look at Lake Crescent.

I no longer yearned for needles to
fashion fear into sackcloth for tearing.
I no longer sensed my mortality
hung by thread.
I suppose, too, my grief
outgrew the talismans.

The table is spare & clean.
A chapter has concluded,
not the disease.
My blood is the altar
and swims.

Sailing in the Sunshine

Somewhere between (determination and will) and (surrender and acceptance) is a sweet spot of flow called letting go. It is softly powerful and within this space is the peaceful present exuding an immediate joy that nothing external nor internal can persuade or interfere with. All is pushed outward except contentment and a gentle inner exaltation. The feeling is, I've won the prize no matter the challenges. The thought is, I've finally figured out the secret to successful survival. No matter what comes, I know, and I mean, *I know*, I will be okay. There is no voice for negativity here, nor fear, overconfidence, or denial. Optimism isn't necessary because, in this space, nothing need be different than it is and will be. And in this knowing that all is as it should be, I am already healed and sailing in the sunshine.

Now I must walk into the reality that persists. Yet, I can recall and reassure, and that will help maintain hope in the questioning that comes.

Filled to the Brim

Like kids giddy in spontaneity
Twenty mostly middle-aged ladies
Gush in transparent turquoise water
Tailing Gulf Stream spotted dolphins,
Our graceless bodies contrast their elegant
Gray-brown dorsal fading to white specks.

We wear masks and breathe through snorkels,
Our relaxed limbs flow willy-nilly,
Thin mammal skin tickling in bubbles.
In twosomes we hold foot-wide handles
Tied to one of two ropes, pulled behind
A catamaran, like the dolphins we converge,

Legs flap and intertwine in the wet wind.
Surging at their speed we watch the impish
Antics of the sublime *Stenella Frontalis,*
Slick, spinning and almost always connecting.
Just one encounter would have filled to the brim
But they remain to swim and weave between us,

For almost an hour they dive and ascend,
Feed on the sea bottom in pearl sand
And like missiles pierce the surface
To arc in living art above the waves.
Our buoy heads bob up and down
To capture every feat they offer like gems.

Sexual beings, a young male turns his belly
Toward the underside of a female as is common
And receives a fluke slap on his face.
He appears to giggle in response
Just five feet below my grasp. I laugh,
Sucking saltwater into my snorkel and mask.

The females draft in offset formation
  As one organism but slightly shingled,
    All of us in propulsion, yet they like magic.
      With their agility, fluidity, and strength
        They seem to float and not project,
          They may stream in the warm current.

The male while still moving hangs submerged
Like an ornament on an invisible branch.
No laws of physics apply to the daimon
As he surveys us and his surroundings
Of the Atlantis-Bimini sanctuary,
Then darts to his best friend in the depths.

    I promised myself I'd swim with dolphins
    After I reached full wellness and remission,
    But now inhale my dream no matter
    The outcome of tests that have no end.
    In my imagination, I plunge with them,
    Exhaling cancer cells as I descend.

        I travel to the larger pod,
        Join in fin dance and song.
        We race through the underwater city,
        Play keep-away with sargassum seaweed,
        Squeak tales of fish-eating festivals
        And heal our scrapes with sonar.

I return to raisin skin and board slowly.
Heavy, my body drips on the vessel
But my oceanic friends linger with me.
Another hour we ogle, aah, and cheer
As the male dolphin vaults to impress us.
Finally, the captain cruises toward dinner.

My hair and hide dry salty in sun's kindness,
Eyes squint from smiling at the setting horizon.
No more air can fit within my expanded lungs
Grown full witnessing the motion of exuberance.
    They also came to watch us, their wild intelligence
    Forty million years older than our scientific sense.

I Can't Go Back

Riffling unfiled records and bills
Somewhat organized in a warped box
I find photos never framed
From a family cruise in 2017,
Examine my unconcerned face—
Posing for cheesy pictures in
Baltic sea ports and evening gowns
Worn once upon a star.
If I could have warned her

This would be the last time
She swing-danced in 3-inch heels with Dad,
Enjoyed white wine with dinner,
Worked out on an elliptical without pain,
Would I tell her, in three years this body
Will betray your assumption,
Take away frivolity, fervent physicality
To hike, run, do yoga, jump,
Freedom to live every day
Without medication
And fear of an earlier death?

Would I have been grateful
If I had known what I would face
Or suffer longer than I have?

When I look into the mirror
Tomorrow morning,
I will warn her of what
She may not know, tell her
Enjoy your plum skin,
Beats, breaths, small pains.
Today's rise to set
May be the worst or best,
Relish your health
As it is.

Homage to My Radiated Hip

I am finally kind to my broken body
when she pops her hip, limps her leg.

I do not shout down my spine
but coo and coax like a loving mother

who bends to kiss the scraped knee.
Held tendons and muscles soften,

quelch their sobs, wipe their eyes.
I push less, soothe with balm

and soak pain in salty water
to lithe what has been burned.

To lithe what has been burned
I soak pain in salty water,

push less, soothe with balm,
quelch my sobs, wipe my eyes.

Held tendons and muscles soften,
bend to kiss the scraped knee,

coo and coax like a loving mother.
I do not shout down my spine

when she pops her hip, limps her leg.
I am finally kind to my broken body.

The Way of Instinct Is to Feed and Grow

Barn swallow vigor
plunges for bugs,
dives and banks,
fights for young

chirping mouths expectant
from rise to set
on the Solstice hours
timed & devoured.

Fly quickly, second & third
broods are coming,
race toward nest fall,
days shortening.

Is this a full turn,
a parenting one?
Now that days caretake
my fledgling body,

sow & nourish
an injured garden,
did my sojourn become
less important?

Late summer dusk
I watch the omens
of rebirth play,
take turns to lift

a paper tissue
off the water,
drop then dive
to catch it.

My Mother's Parents Free Ranged

Mimaw and Pawpaw farmed their own vegetables, harvested nuts and apples, grazed cattle, and kept chickens in Alabama. A creek encircled their acreage, and they pumped and piped their water from a springhouse. Oh, how simple it all seems now. Simple it could be, should I live in a rural setting as was theirs, work consistently on the land, hands rough, back aching from bending into aging. City dwellers rely on convenience, the hidden cruelty, wastefulness, and carbon costs considerable. What my grandparents did not grow or make they bought from nearby neighbors. Clean living. Purpose direct and basic.

The land was not first theirs. They earned its respect over time, though, hoeing and resowing, taking in boarders, sharing their abundance from rich soil. They invited me to come, stay longer. The farm calmed from its labor. I reflect that when young, I didn't enjoy shucking corn, snapping peas, and cracking walnuts. I didn't realize an idle body sours the mind. It was much later that I appreciated dipping my fingers into moist dirt, its blanket softness and mineral scent awakening elements within dormant knowing cells, enlivening them, retracing my roots. Perhaps this is what my body desires now—to plant her hands into earth, draw basic needs into her veins, feed the chickens, and rejoin the unbroken circle.

Does Grief Die?

Last week, I learned a friend died.
I know why she didn't tell
Anyone outside her family
She was succumbing to cancer.

Why would we want others
To mourn us while living?

I search, have misplaced
My sadness at her passing.
Facing death, I'm not surprised
When someone proceeds me.

Am I shocked out,
Dead to tragedy?
If I cry for her,
Will I keep crying for me?

I'm sure that when those
Most close to me depart
I again will find grief clawing.
Still, death seems less crushing.

Mortality doesn't take away loved ones
But transcends us into our truest selves,
The closer we are to the glass door of death
The freer we are to cornerstone live.

Should I outlive my parents
I will rejoice in tearful thirst
Knowing they didn't quit
Mourning their youngest.

The definition of death
Has turned on its fuzzed head,
I no longer draw a line where life ends
And where grief begins.

A Life Worth Remembering

Ice begat me, severed me from granite mother. Tumbled me from brothers, deposited me jagged on a slide where I seasoned many years in snow and sun. I roofed a chattering pika, then a squeaky marmot, until a sheep knocked me downward. I hung a long while in a high valley lake that froze and melted, breaking me smaller. A big snow year rolled me on the bottom, dropped me over a waterfall where I bounced too many times to count. I broke again, a brilliant jade revealed and polished every year as river's current swept me along, no time to grow algae.

For a couple of years, fish had me watch over their young. I followed them swimming into wider waterways and we encountered salt. They freed into the Pacific, but waves pushed me back to shore where I rumbled and popped with others, rounded and flattened, gathered into lather, plied by tides, until one day I lay near a barren log and sunned, motionless, old, and rested. Micro bits dissolved away every day in the rain, wind, and rays. I shined bright green when wet, a dull sage when dry. Days blurred into eons of continuous shushing next to ocean. I lulled until it stormed. Some friends slid underneath one another. I was exposed for hundreds of years, I gather. Many four- and two-legged–beings moved about and stepped on me, shifting my position.

Then, almost suddenly, smooth skin grabbed me, turned me over, scraped my sister against me, slivers escaping the torture. But I remained, becoming sharp once more. Tied to a stick with cedar bark, I speared flesh, hit bone and chipped off, toppled into a bay, settled under waves and deteriorated to pebbles nudged by nibbling fish. Eventually I dispersed in tiny specks, washed ashore again, touched more land than I thought possible in one life. I sighed as sand across the beach miles. Softened my radiance, sunk, and absorbed into cooler layers dropping ever downward into earth. And I recalled how I began, how my mother formed millions of years ago in the sea, lifted up and up into the piercing air, her children underneath her skirt, awaiting birth and adventure.

Salmon Parenting

after Kevin Talbot's photograph, "Homeward Bound"

It's an ancient beckoning,
this return to birthplace,
struggle to replace ourselves
in the circle of Earth story,
give our deterioration to
the next generation.

Sea swimming, the individual joy
of being a free salmon,
is the most romantic notion
of this life, feeding.
But the journey home,
fight to fertilize,
is tomorrow's prosperity.

We dissolve into gravel,
no eyes to witness the progression
of alevin to fry, smolt to adult,
nor how our offspring
favor their parents, whose fat,
muscle, and organs burned for
energy in their creation.

Spawning is an act of faith
in our dying process.
Pure sacrifice, unknown outcomes
without regret nor nurturing interference.
Impact is finned like a relay baton.

My run is done,
make yours count, children,
carry coho on,
nourish yourself and everything,
for salmon feed the rivers, the fungus,
lift into clouds, rain to land.
Our legacy is richest
just before and after death.

Hugging Alder

Many humans visit my point on the edge of Lake Crescent at the mouth of Barnes Creek, which flows more like a river, I think. They pose for cameras, throw rocks across the water's calming surface as the sun begins to set behind what's called Aurora Ridge. Sometimes they sit, lean against me, or the little ones hang from my lower limbs. But there is one, a woman comparable to my age in human years, who presses one foot against an offshoot at my base and carefully lifts herself to perch on my level branch. She rubs the ribs of my wrinkled bark, picks at my lichen, and pats me with her hand, her love. I can feel it, you know, the light releasing into my marrow. I think we share a beginning story. I feel the water in her well, we all carry similar ruminating material in our cells. We share golden moments in sun's setting warmth until the ball of flame hides behind the range. One day, she spots one carving in particular, humans like to knife their marks, make me weep until I slowly scab. She traces a finger over the letters a man and woman created together. She whispers, 'I'm sorry that they've done this to you.' I've healed those cuts yet her words soothe something deep, which speaks of human loss that's rubbed off on me, like the lichen. Later, one of the couple returns and notches these numbers next to their lines: '81-'23. I can't wait to show the woman. Sure enough, she notices, and I feel her joy dim. She says, 'It has ended, a life or a marriage perhaps.' She hugs herself closer to my trunk. We weep together for the couple, for loss, for time passing. We cry into the growing dark and cold. We hold the water and scars of one another.

With Thanks

Thank you, Finishing Line Press and my editor, Christen Kincaid, for sharing my poems with a larger community of readers. I want to thank fellow writers who regularly review, validate, and critique my work. I would not have dealt with my health challenges or healed as well without writing about my feelings and experiences, then sharing them with you. Thanks, Kelly, for serving as my cancer patient sounding board, and Kelsey and Mary Ellen, for providing ongoing feedback.

I am grateful to Gary Copeland Lilley who has encouraged me to "bring it" in writing workshop since 2021. Thanks to Linda and Heidi of Olympic Peninsula Authors for their dedication to and promotion of writers. I have valued learning from workshop instructors through the Port Townsend Writers Conference: Alice Derry, Holly J. Hughes, Claudia Castro Luna, CMarie Fuhrman, Matthew Olzmann, and Tess Gallagher. Thank you, Kelli Russell Agodon and Annette Spaulding-Convy for your *Two Sylvias Weekly Muse*, generative workshops, and online community. Thank you, Sandra Yannone, for your generous introductions on Cultivating Voices LIVE Poetry. I am also thankful for collaborations with poet and curator Agnes Bourne, whose recognition of my earlier work spurred my poetry's growth more quickly.

I am especially indebted to *TulipTree Review*, for enough confidence in my work to award me a Merit Prize and Pushcart Prize nomination, and to *OncoLink.org* of Penn Medicine for an ongoing venue for my cancer poems.

Many hugs to the healthcare and complementary health professionals who have assisted and continue to assist me. Thank you, family, friends, and prayer angels who listen to, support, and pray for me. Much love to Mike, Mom, Dad, Leigh, Luke, Jake, and Mike's family. I thank God every day for my life and well-being.

Laura E. Garrard is a poet and artist living in Port Angeles, Washington. She is also a CranioSacral Therapist, an outdoors recreationist, and a citizen scientist. She grew up in an adventurous family that left the South, lived on the East Coast, and then the West. They explored beloved National Parks on vacation. Garrard's father told his two daughters tent-time stories based on the histories of these places. On these trips, Garrard wrote nature poetry. Her first poems were published in children's anthologies and in a local California newspaper.

In college, Garrard studied advertising and public relations (Texas Christian) and news-editorial journalism (University of Tennessee). Her master's project utilized in-depth interviews with two women, one white and one Black, who were the first in their families to earn college degrees in 1960s South. She reported as an intern for a newspaper in Knoxville before moving to Nashville, where she pursued employment in publishing. Garrard became assistant editor for a collaborative imprint between Country Music Foundation Press and Vanderbilt University Press, and managed an encyclopedia project published by Oxford University. She served as assistant editor, production manager, and a writer for *The Journal of Country Music.* For over ten years, Garrard worked as an independent proofreader for Rutledge Hill Press and Thomas Nelson Books.

Adventure called her West again, this time to Jackson, Wyoming. There she opened her own complementary health practice and focused on time outdoors, writing, and painting. In addition to showing art, she contributed poetry and prose to local publications. During the pandemic, her bodywork practice was temporarily shut down. As she reopened it, Garrard sought aid for hip discomfort and received a jolting blood cancer diagnosis, a plasmacytoma. This eventually progressed into multiple myeloma. Her husband accepted a job on the Olympic Peninsula, and they moved to new mountains. Garrard found supportive writing groups, through which she developed her poetry, now published nationally and internationally.

Her health has been well-managed, yet her radiated hip has limited her mobility. Garrard has spoken against ableism and discrimination toward cancer patients through her poetry. Her poem, "Homage to My Radiated

Hip," was selected as a finalist in *Bellevue Literary Review*'s John & Eileen Allman Prize for Poetry, and "Hugging Alder" was awarded a Merit Prize and Pushcart Prize nomination by *TulipTree Review*. You may also read her work in *The Madrona Project, Amethyst Review, Silver Birch, Tidepools, The Orchards Poetry Journal, Pangyrus, The Journal of Expressive Writing,* and her series "Poetry That Fits" on Penn Medicine's *OncoLink.org*.

LauraEGarrard.com

www.ingramcontent.com/pod-product-compliance
Lightning Source LLC
LaVergne TN
LVHW090540110826
845146LV00003B/1189

* 9 7 9 8 8 9 9 9 0 3 8 1 6 *